With *Black Box Syndrome* Jose-Luis Moctezuma reveals himself to be one of the finest contemporary poets of risk. Thinking past probabilistic risk analysis, this book enlivens older and outlasting speculative analytics such as fate, fortune, divination, and influence. Built from the computational concept of the black box (a system known only by its inputs and outputs) and the structural poetics of the I Ching, this book tangles with the inescapably vulgar qualities of uncertainty: prefrontal cortex, financial instruments, divinatory practices, global supply chains, dream horizons, paranoiac demographics, and pre-nodal subjects. In a startling collection of hexagram poems, Moctezuma's Black Box Syndrome discloses the sigil hidden in the vulgarity of chance, that is, poetry always.

—Edgar Garcia, author of *Skins of Columbus: A Dream Ethnography*

In its formal constriction, Jose-Luis Moctezuma's *Black Box Syndrome* triggers torrents of lyric profusion. Nervy and nutritive, this is the black box as cosmic mysterium, optic macula and nourishing milpa, cunning and exact in its cycles of pliancy and rest. Like the dream machines Clare and Blake confected against the crises of enclosure and industrialization, Moctezuma's black boxes form a marvelous anti-mechanism against all forms of supremacist thought.

—Joyelle McSweeney, author of *Toxicon and Arachne*

T0270188

Dream-workings, plastivores, military lingo, an economics of exorbitance, war, torture, computation, a theogony in music, visual and acoustical repetitions, incantation, murmuration, a poetry of graceful removal, of closed-circuit telepathy: in Jose-Luis Moctezuma's remarkable *Black Box Syndrome*, the poet, availing a trickster's shapeshifting commitments, discovers how "narratives of miscreancy are common where the yolk of the sun splatters" in this series of austere, mysterious, and relentlessly intelligent poems that show his readers a total ideogrammic plan for the chaos magic needed to face the machinery of our harrowing present.

—Peter O'Leary, author of *The Hidden Eyes of Things*

During the coronavirus pandemic, life became remote; consciousness, stripped of somatic partnership, was trimmed to the size of a Zoom square. The poems of *Black Box Syndrome* articulate the traumas (and revelations) of such constraint in a new Book of Changes, where the technological present grips the fingers of the ancients and pulls them into their algorithmic rooms. Each synthetic hexagram sizzles with a fusion of influences in "closed circuit telepathy." Electric and mesmeric, this book will explode your brain in the best way.

—Jena Osman, author of *Motion Studies*

Black Box Syndrome

Cover design by Jose-Luis Moctezuma
Cover art from Gottfried Wilhelm Leibniz, Wikipedia Commons, Robert Fludd
and John Haslam, Wellcome Collection

Interior design by Laura Joakimson and Jose-Luis Moctezuma
Cover typeface: Lora
Interior typeface: Lora and Futura

Library of Congress Cataloging-in-Publication Data

Library of Congress Cataloging-in-Publication Data

Names: Moctezuma, Jose-Luis, 1981- author.
Title: Black box syndrome / Jose-Luis Moctezuma.
Description: Oakland, California : Omnidawn Publishing, 2023. | Summary:
  "Black Box Syndrome is a series of poems (or "black boxes") based on the
  hexagrams in the I Ching. Following the aleatoric tradition popularized
  by the surrealists and extended by the work of John Cage and Jackson
  Maclow, the poems cast their assorted lenses (or coins, or yarrow
  stalks) at the hazards of the incessant financialization of everyday
  life. Synthesizing chance-operational aesthetics with Aztec anatomical
  science, conspiracy theory with systems theory, and the black box model
  with the concept of the "influencing machine," Black Box Syndrome
  articulates the tension between lyric excess and digital compaction that
  encodes poetic discourse in the age of pandemic. Over and against the
  corrosive world-shrinking effects of Wall Street risk management and
  futures trading, the black boxes in this book propose a
  counter-divination that distorts, deranges, and decolonizes the logic of
  empire"-- Provided by publisher.

Identifiers: LCCN 2023019334 | ISBN 9781632431226 (trade paperback)
Subjects: LCGFT: Experimental poetry.
Classification: LCC PS3613.O29 B57 2023 | DDC 811/.6--dc23/eng/20230523
LC record available at https://lccn.loc.gov/2023019334

Published by Omnidawn Publishing, Oakland, California
www.omnidawn.com
10 9 8 7 6 5 4 3 2 1
ISBN: 978-1-63243-122-6

Black Box Syndrome

Jose-Luis Moctezuma

OMNIDAWN PUBLISHING
OAKLAND, CALIFORNIA
2023

TABLE OF CONTENTS

"When you will have made him a body without organs,
then you will have delivered him from all his automatic reactions
and restored him to his true freedom"

■   Antonin Artaud, *To Have Done with the Judgment of God*

"I will have built two small boxes.
I put small things in the boxes,
A sign explains the boxes to any-
one who should approach them.
It says 'Meaningless work boxes.'
Throw all of the things into one
box, then throw all of the things
into the other. Back and forth,
back and forth. Do this for as long
as you like. What do you feel?
Yourself? The Box? The Things?
Remember this doesn't mean any-
thing."

■   Walter de Maria, *Project for Boxes*
      (from *An Anthology of Chance Operations*, 1963)

"Black Box Syndrome: A general term for the problems that may arise in using complex mathematical and statistical models in finance. For example, it may be difficult to model transparently the impacts of trading on the overall exposure of a complicated set of positions."

■   OxfordReference.com

"The schizophrenic influencing machine is a machine of mystical nature. The patients are able to give only vague hints of its construction. It consists of boxes, cranks, levers, wheels, buttons, wires, batteries, and the like. Patients endeavor to discover the construction of the apparatus by means of their technical knowledge, and it appears that with the progressive popularization of the sciences, all the forces known to technology are utilized to explain the functioning of the apparatus. All the discoveries of mankind, however, are regarded as inadequate to explain the marvelous powers of this machine, by which the patients feel themselves persecuted."

■   Victor Tausk, "On the Origin of the 'Influencing Machine' in Schizophrenia"

open close open close open close open close open close open close
what's in the box what's   the password why are they
brain-sayings fluid-locking thigh-talking bomb-bursting tying-down
looking inside the vapors   are sending me outside the
kiteing stomach-skinning lobster-cracking lengthening of the brain
surface there is depth or   a machine to rule them all

17

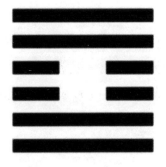

"Seminal fluid, male and female—effluvia of copper—ditto of sulphur—
the vapours of vitriol and aqua fortis—ditto of nightshade and
hellebore—effluvia of dogs—stinking human breath—putrid effluvia—
ditto of mortification and of the plague—stench of the sesspool—gaz
from the anus of the horse—human gaz—gaz of the horse's greasy
heels—Egyptian snuff [(((*dream-workings*))]—vapour and effluvia of
arsenic—poison of toad—otto of roses and of carnation."

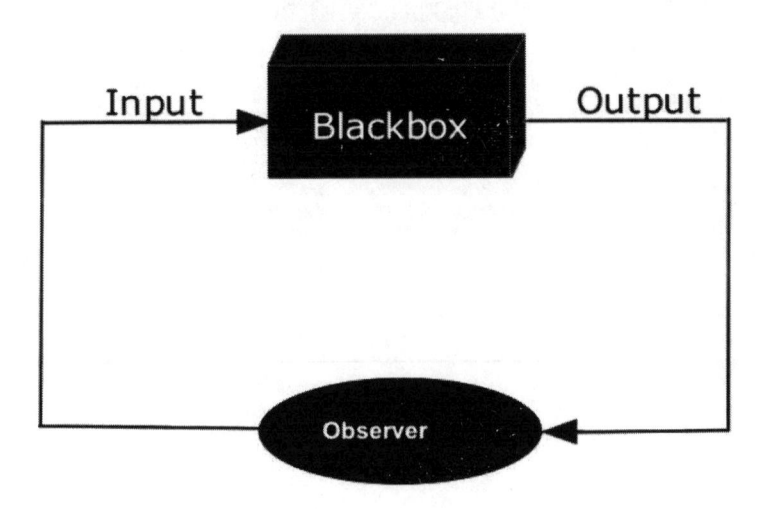

0

inside the mind a box and inside the box
a word and inside the word several letters
and inside the letters sounds and inside
the sounds a bird call and inside the call
a shadow and inside the shadow a voice
and inside the voice a name and inside
the name a trace and inside the trace a
grassblade and inside the blade a color
and inside red there is blood and inside
blood there is a stream and inside river
there are murmurs and inside the echo
a hand and in the palm another hand
and it pulls you downward and beneath
the downward there is breath there are
choruses there are four walls there are
acoustics there are waves and geometries
there are figures on the wall and lanterns
outside there is a wind at the door then
the eye opens and there is a chasm and
inside the chasm there is a mirror and
in the mirror there are murmurations
and inside murmuration there are star-
lings and in the starling there is mind
and inside the mind the body again &
and then the organs and then the box

I

a flux of changes to the timeframe disjoints the specter on its flightplan
but i am here ((inside the lung)) attuned to frequencies of wind pattern
it startles me how the evening bleeds the day of blood on a quiet street
a tongue of indifference strokes the inertia that settles in each behavior
solid as pungent smoke ((or humid arbor)) it smells my edge of shadow
an ambuscade deforms my shapeliness and i leap into the milpa to hide

II

the difference between hoar frost and frost is romantic vapor
we balanced the checkbooks and squared the rigidity of circles
the difference between were wolves and wolves is retrocession
for ex if you move this way the polyp appears to shed metal
the cards told them to cease yet they dared to dream of a box
whence foxgloves rise like moons in trypophobic lavender

III

the air loom weaves its theory   they can't sculpt the clay in wind
did you ever note how the objects in the world disappear in the cracks
a black box sutures them   a zipper that tenderly seals the lip
other things need explanans   like the anatomy of a derivative
magic is in the can opener   and yet we do not see its violence
our theory of things is that we are submerged in radiowave and we sing

IV

we sing our punishments into being & there are seven heads behind us
a machine to influence minds   exists as a fig in the mind that's
the trick how the breath en-   jambs the "factitious airs" into
expression and suddenly "the   feels" peel away into affects we
can touch and dismantle and replace with a stalactite force of absence
there is no world here only   the emptiness of 382 characters

V

i am waiting in the distant   country she is waiting in a letter
the child is waiting to receive the letter but a grammar of cages prevents
its syntax to formulate an   understanding beyond what the
body needs in a privation of technologies of self: clean water soap walls
waiting for distant relations to arrive and paper and a system for paper
the world is too much with us too much because it consists in enclosure

VI

a gloved woman opens the box and unloosens a sprig of gold mimosa
a cyborg's orgasm wakes her up from vivid dreams of apple curvature
a machine for chaos syncs up our lactic naturecultures in social secrecy
erasmus denied fault for it   he sells vacuums & malfunctions
it was his fault instead the one who is always late to yesterday's seances
it was no box nor leathern   belt it was blue mint in a bell jar

VII

birds in the magnetic fields   spell evil of a pristine liquidity
black ink in clean spearmint   the air loom might be outside
i feel my brain sweat within   when i hear my own breathing
a man named bill worms in-   side the mind's encampments
mezcal is nothing like this these shakes this gouty toe festering throat
there should be a syntax for   avian flu to guard against -noia

VIII

let the breast be full of sincerity
a gesture toward univocality something
from pigmentation and distilled
there must be people out there
of what constitutes the palaver
while i lie here in the milpa and

as the earthenware of black soil
like a caged mind turned soft
in kith and cabbage and fishgut
beyond the kiting of my heart
in a sequence of migrant geese
stare out in a teachable silence

IX

a return from an exile of cunning and kaleidoscopes of tauromachy
the scientist fake-news the fashionable idea of electrical fascination
as if anything electrical auto-   matically meant the mesmeric
but what's really happening is that sisyphus doesn't understand what's
happening and a strap beneath is slowly removed and a strap beneath
him is gradually removed and a strap under you is gracefully removed

X

there are no errors treading the adumbrated pathways no errors level
with the road that leads from joy's calvary to depressions of star anise
perched stark naked on a stress of sugar cane browned in solar plexus
i'm reminded of the forgetful one   the one who treaded on a tiger
its tail flickering in night heat who sank in a quicksand of slow dying
the gradient fang a foresight of the tropic thrusting him into brutal life

XI

grass pulled up from its source   code like city walls submerged
in governance of green water   and the moat like a shimmering
stagnation in their abridged lust   magnetic fluids between hands
held in republican splendor while they counterplot minor conspiracies
the anonymous feel of a hand pressed in another and the giving in to
a universalized harmony like vocables in a syntax of bright premises

XII

so when it starts calamities of thought are pushed back from the edge
and folded over like napkins in your lap and the suggestion-apparatus
winds up the bells and whistles and the ornaments that speak in wind
shame unwraps in my breast   when i begin to think i am not
me here speaking but someone   else gripping my brain as if it
were a hand gripping another   or a picture moving in my head

XIII

the nahual hides its arms in thick grass under various moons of inquest
a brother animal breathes in the machine vapor and asks that the blood
of a running brook offer to spill its redblack over stones broken by light
in the red east they say the belated one married her who opened the box
my tonalli returns me to him   and he is me in the undercurrent
narratives of miscreancy are common where the yolk of the sun splatters

XIV

they are in love with narrative and large wagons custom built for largesse
the poem is a machine which   should make sense and carry loads
the black box is a machine which should contaminate the air with feeling
a dementia like the aroma of mictlan in the gushing of pomegranate seed
our rapt faces in the screentime ennature the eagle gourd's washed heart
he wondered of the wandering tribes who still speak inside disorientation

XV

the telephone erects semblances   in the way our shared mind lifts
paranoias for an excess of sight   across mute channels of speech
he is caught off guard when the   call comes out of a vacuum in
a corner of the grotto and the sense of day or night is blurred in bell
song while the voice asks him to   illustrate the levers and buttons
which the imagination conjures   to ward off the not not-knowing

XVI

a theogony in music might appear   irrelevant to what words
manifest in the shape of eclipses   as stark as the black dog
the spheres make their displeasure known in silver metal machine music
an om in double triangle unlocks   huitzilopochtli's huehuetl
the mallet strikes several ghost   notes on an ocelot spine
yet he lives w/o dying his dark   mind devoted to harmony

XVII

the purple sun extinguishes   on the remains of a cane toad
the consulting firm instructs us to ingest it during company retreats
a crisis of management might be offset by opioids of fact-checking
object permanence quakes   their eyelids blink in sedition
what is an individual under   the lens of closed-circuit tele-
pathy or the adherents of red poppy seed smooth like saliva on skin

XVIII

so the essence of the mind is its spirit which we call the brain shroud
the medium of a medium   in the medium of a leaf pattern
a grande or a medium size   or a medium cool watch party
it just takes a switch to light up the abrasions on the penal colonists
the mind body divide or the nature culture divide or a biblical lesson
cannot convert these men   into bright automata we desire

XIX

what is an individual under   the scrutiny of the black box
a dummy's guide to leaping   into leprosies of yellowy faith
the mother wakes up from   auto-suggestion   asphyxiation
yet i undo my father's work   tying the doll's loose shoelace
the pre-oedipal capitalizes on the phantom logic of yggdrasil branch
arboreal patterns and the camouflage of filial relation are called 401k

XX

a woman looks out from the sliver of a door ajar in a way that hides
the configuration of the machine metaphoring into a discrete series

curiouser and curiouser the Q   in the question or the doxxing
of the anonymous in signal jam   white rabbit noise in the bush
the conspiratorial spaceways   or what fictions pleaseth you
a gamification of communitas   in the steady leakage of cipher

XXI

his feet are in the stocks and he is deprived of his toes and he bites soft

on the goose flesh that he learns   is actually his in a false eucharist

waterboarding and scopic drives and the history of the neo-inquisition

harass him at each bedlam turn   a war under reason's sun is war

on reason this is what's called   cogito ergo sum to be deprived

of one's tongue of one's ears of one's neck wearing the cangue to think

XXII

the witness testified that he had hired mail-coach after mail-coach with
an exorbitant confidence in his   credit card to foot the bill in step
with games of deception called   espionage a "national organ" for
"mighty events" and the glories of acceleration which stir our idealism
for communes and atopias like   no place in the world we dwell
as in a mountain and inside the mountain fire and inside the fire speed

XXIII

the captive finds himself substituted by sudden apparitions of people
carrying his wares from the left   to the right hemisphere of time
what his left hand holds is what   the right hand obviates in silence
for ex a painting of a black cube   in white space or garden variety
gardens for ex a picture of black   boxes containing each other in-
divisibly for ex a silver monolith   in a utah canyon falling over &

XXIV

he recalls his "form" when he
and sees himself sculpted in time
the imago comes to life and it's
like a treadmill or the hamster's
a temporal lobe interrupted by

gives in to the messaging cues
or muybridged by zoetropes
a box that has learned to talk
agon with pinions and wheels
being in many places at once

orientates what the right knows of the left in a flourishing of prayer

XXV

how do we know it is documentary or nonfiction how we do split hairs
on this magnitude if we are bacteria on a god's fingernail how do boxes
work at sunrise or dusk how do we know the cat is alive or in my brain
how does the internet of things   work versus the world of things
if the doorbell rings why do they   need to see my face looking out
at its face if the door is locked but in my phantasy it is always unlocked

XXVI

a daemon in the engine of memory & its matrix a mystic writing pad
erasing and unerasing the pivot   from oracle into apprehension
the latticework describes a plot   an influencer weaves in oxygen
they ask him to draw it out and he does so by holding his breath long
enough that it stops working underground the rattle of its barrels and
tubes and battery life at low tide the seacoast erasing the sand's script

XXVII

you look at me till your lower jaw hangs down and sits there on its hinge
objects in the mirror are closer   than they appear in the mind's eye
turn on the channel to number   zero or patient zero hides in static
the dogs at the door or behind   the gate are agents of the imaginary
she's telling me they're almost   here so i lock the gate and the creak
is almost too much to withstand the flatness of the earth weighs me down

XXVIII

things are placed on the ground   & on the ground a woven mat is set

the patchwork of roots drinks longingly in the dark spot of incorporation

the organic myth is beautiful during a time of cicadas & we laugh out loud

seeing our bodies in x-ray our fragility a thing we forget in haste and rage

the technical fortitude of a cell tower what does it matter when we dry up

if the marsh hides fossils or   tupelo & willow patterns at sundown

XXIX

he enters a lime cavern in the   mountain and listens to ghost
songs travel along the channels of the rockwork and its blue arteries
feed back loops that intensify   in an echo of lost whippoorwills
intoxication pounds his heart   open and heavy as bag-torn rice
he is defeated by the machine he is its proxy it retreats behind his eyes
the pastoral world recalls him   back to organism back to the box

XXX

and went down to the white world and glimpsed the savage elisions
a declining sun fulminant   in lengthy shade of its demise
if he could be controlled by a tube he wouldn't have it any other way
espionage and mind games and poetry keep a same energy in what's
visible at the core of speech   yet the interzone exists at all
because time is the evil and our creationisms are fictions on the box

XXXI

i want to believe that its dusk   holds warm temperature inside
the calves of its legs measure a caprice of the mind possessed by love
the love of a gadfly imprinted in vellum the love of whiteness printed
on the face of time on the bald spot of mont blanc romance of many
dimensions a boolean method   for containing her amours in-
ward and outward & their love   for sigils engendering a codex

XXXII

there is freedom in restriction   they tell us there is freedom
in austerity to be in a box on   the edge of a profound gulf
an evergreen ever given in deciduous poetic whose lyric is privacy
a song of the self in real time or IRL or blown up & zoomed upon
by cameras of infinitesimal erection and scopic drives retconned by
multiverses blocked up by ships   on the artificed shore of suez

XXXIII

so we are drawn back by seven people behind us behind you and me
of being numerous the crash test dummy crouches in cruel optimism
a sleeping father perishes in the image his child makes of him snoring
an automaton springs to life and dances in the constraint of a room
the yggdrasil in yellow river   like oxhide born in the factory
sucks the world of its water &   secures its society in the milpa

XXXIV

he looks out on the shining   pathways that lead from Z
to A, searching the sacred   Julia who lisps in the rhythm
of algae, her heart corded in the mitre of various disjecta membra
power is the song in the murmuration no one thing singular in the
milpa ((the cordoned field ribboned off from the mass as the velvet
of her inner skin cordons the coffin of her breast from night airs))

XXXV

a sun rising in the western mirror reopens the closed portals of speech
my words fly like beacons   alighting on the mountain ridge
"the grammarians encode their bile in translations of operating manuals"
but what i really want to   know is how do they transform
their livers into humidifiers   secreting gaseous memories into
the membrane of a worm   lodged in the valve of my tongue

XXXVI

the light darkens as he shifts   to the left side of the belly of

xibalba and a woman wears   fingerless gloves as she digitates

the levers of his desiring-   machine its circumference thick

the leather of a belt pressuring and lathering him on his warm-hued

thighs lovemarked chanced   into submission the intrauterine

recollected in tranquility the full shaft a sheer genitality of the machine

XXXVII

the wind in the fire fans the seeds that father the family resemblances
i dream of a headless woman and she is the mother they tell me she is
the vestige of ancestral traumas   borne by a tlatoani whose hair
she pulled and gripped his tonalli as it flew from him chasing a snake
the mind is a place i retire to   far away from the influencing
machine which sends fire drills and breathes iyotl on me and my kin

XXXVIII

my feelings for a horse i would trade my feelings for a perfect body
the strength of an automobile   the vigor of a stallion in heat
i see my body like a sarcophagus placed far away from me and some
one ((or there are seven))   perform their ingenuity on it
i am stimulated here and down there i am electrified the wheels turn
a fire in the lake perturbs me my body is a switch in someone's hand

XXXIX

language isn't enough to share   these trivial feelings with you
an obstruction between the tongue and the roof of my mouth exists
a barrier is placed between my   mind and the voice that speaks
inside me the borderline is a fiction in the book i write and yet people
continue to suffer the anguish   of not crossing from one end
to the other there is a guard here & he says he's now closing the gate

XL

come under this red rock   they say the shadow is a place of
moisture or perhaps blood   my father delivers me from non-
sense when i serve him the bowl and suddenly i am a father of nations
the magician will write of me   and label my conquests destiny
the black box predicts stocks will rise the oceans will rise plastic islands
will rise the temperatures will   rise a million migrant boats too

XLI

i want to believe that at the foot of the mountain there is a lake and
at the foot of the lake there are   craters that drink of the lake
and drink of the mountain slow-   ly amicably like a vampire bat
that kisses the throat with kind-   ness its love as dark as the in-
side of a blackberry now glittering now cloud-shadow in the ravine
flowing through the mind a sigil wrapped inside words inside codex

XLII

the great water meets me where the mountain ends and the nahual
counsels me to cross it in spite of the box's infernal commandment
i must increase with the hyacinths   i must grow with the dahlias
my organism is still mine is it not   i dream of it when it flees me
when the box conjures my spirit   i stroke its hair and cradle it
songs of the self are total bullshit my phallus grows w/ or w/o me

XLIII

& maybe it does deflate and fall   down when i have finished loving
the self underneath cameras of infinite loving grace their pistils gleaming
the corollaries to the corollas hidden in the fold of an eyelid closed and
thinking of a naked sunset falling lushly on decapitated mountaintops &
coalblack in a hush of starlings that layer the errata of glacial turpitude &
transport me to an alterity that hums and murmurs of boxes & boxes &

XLIV

the form that fish in a tank make under fluorescent light invisibilizes
them, much like a melon covered in willow leaf, or the sensation of
running into a wall when the sky brightens, a plastiglomerate effect
in which gills and scales and debris are plasticized into a new atomic
arrangement, under water where the light breaks up and leaks in oily
patterns and microplastic   particles emerge break merge

XLV

a gathering of the trillion assets   a magic carpet array of debts
& derivatives, where deconstructions cling like tetrapods on the coast
they manage risk as wind manages erosion, sealing heaven from earth's
resentment, conspiracy of breath   a breathing-together of those
who spy on us from space, the so-   called plutonians, who wager
psychiatric success, at high tide   memorizing complots for song

XLVI

within the earth the wood   surges and blooms in moisture
in the wood the honeycomb   learns of the wax moth's larvae
in the honeycomb the bee   agonizes over the parasitic nest
what pushes upward are plastic islands skimming the surface tension
a sea skater allocates its zooplankton and collects polyethylene instead
plastivores relieve the earth   & the wood whorls in seawater

XLVII

the box in actuality is empty   emptier than the stone lake
where a wounded king seeks godhead but the fish does not come
the framers of events testify to the glories of modernism but move-
ment only brings remorse ill-   will scandal casuistry sinful
thoughts the oppression of the forgetful – habeas corpus is a myth
to keep us in the funhouse   where each mirror is broken

XLVIII

we might think of the box   as a kind of wellspring in which
the rope and bucket descend & descend and the floor is never reached
a distant sound of waterdrops   rises in the air in a temperature
that conceals the color in the grate that keeps the inside from the out
a hairpin made of trinitite or fordite clasps a lock of hair that i threw
into the well which doesn't   change only my memory of her

XLIX

today i sing praises to a medlar   sprouting in germinal fever
yesterday i lyricized the juniper rioting in the meadowlands and to-
morrow i think of a messianic harvest bringing its thermidor & re-
call conservation efforts by partisans who jumped vineyards to dis-
pute the quality of my vintage   but i'm drunk again with fog
the snow and sleet pressure me into belief in this new world order

L

the iphone warms my hand and the sphericity of its cauldron heals me
the finger sensor from delhi   acknowledges me and the circuit
board from taipei and taoyuan recognizes me when i unlock the screen
shipped from suwon south korea the semiconductor from hsinchu talks
to me about its day and i console it reminding it of its camera cousin in
santa clara the mic from shen-   zhen interrupts & asks me to stop

LI

the supply chain is an allegory for the ways the black box breaks
down our collective phantasies concerning the borderlands and
its intangible affects there is no "here" and there is no "there" there are
no states which are united in us or in the language we speak there
is no identity crisis other than the dark core of HMM Algeciras
ambling blindly along the mystic canals of panama in search of interval

LII

stacks as mountains on mountains the containers multiply the plateaus
stacked one upon the other   as hierarchies or principalities
enthroning the kingdom of   this world and its citadels em-
balming the historicity of fragments and the erasure of the change be-
yond change a stillness like   the gaze of an arctic sun on the
corpse of an emaciated white   bear having sung itself to sleep

LIII

the wild goose's fidelity is like that of the wind embracing the valleys
of the mountain they promised me pen and paper and draughtsmen
and yet here i still wait for my   tea at three behind iron bars
i will school myself the ways of the mage it only takes indeliberation
the nonthinking thoughtless   thought discarded knowledge
like loose paper scraps ((is its   own sexuality & becomes law))

LIV

they warn me that a magnetic-   fluid-impregnated russian comes
armed with an arsenal of white   magic tricks dubbed cambridge
analytica and assorted psyops and brain-sayings that will bring certain
nations into a reflexive order   they call speculative realism or
an anti-somatism that we shall title a physics of the AI privileging the
mechanical bride over and against her suitors WTF were they anyway

LV

the assassins believe in the   rights of man forsooth they've
invented the body so why   not push this strawman before
me as a conviction procedure alongside puppet shows of abundance
but all things are in abundance look around you all things are speaking
to you from the inner core   of teyolia the heart of the heart
of a cannulated cow who listens to the rumblings of its intestinal truth

LVI

coronavirus roves the spaceways and we are its inhabitants in this black
box they call sein und zeit   our vagrant breath contaminates
the dialectical channels with objective correlatives or prosthetic pathos
death does not let me go it warns me that it has hacked my smarthome
from its shining distance   such things are possible: plastic
flowers astroturf nomadic   tamagotchi roombas in the wild

LVII

the wind bloweth where it listeth sourceless as what occurs in black box
systemanalyse und programmentwicklung supplies supply chain cockpits
cloud-based the monitors stylize   the time horizons for a hotel suite
of operations running the gamut from defecation to waste management
to localvore economies such as faster one-click purchase of assault rifles
for all your hunting proclivities   and schizo-patriotic-individuation

LVIII

today they've released me at last   i'm tasked with bookkeeping
the library of babble contains books that all speak of the black cube
the world the flesh and the devil are all one in paradise as the angels
a future of feeling in our throats   rendering   unto   buonaparte
the good bits the fatty acids the stench of skin that soothes the soul
reminders of the old world the old sex while we interzone in ecstasy

LIX

a dream of daedalus in the end cancels out the dooms of icarus i was
told once that everything dissipates no matter how darkened the heart
of the box may be there is no-   thing to fear in the death posture
the entropic lettering of my   name and my organs speak out
against the empires of permanence the flippant automatisms that fluid-
lock us and lengthen our brain   vats the bombs burst to unleash

LX

pandaemonium is a film by   william blake about the coming
of the machine ((or was it the night mail)) in eveningtide when church
bells vanish like a forest fire   that leaps into the lake and swims
our current philosophy of   necrophilia relies on algorhythms
that reanimate the dead in holograms required to perform 1990s hits
we lie between prometheus and epimetheus as sterile as tears in rain

LXI

i speak with the pigs and the fishes i open my heart to them and lay
bare the inner truths that disassemble me at night & reassemble me
at daybreak when there is no   box and i see only skyward
the cranes flying toward the   east and white eggs hatching
in the wake of perfect quietude like the silence of god when he naps
my heart is full when i leave it out & the rain collects & i drink deep

LXII

and even when the box closes   and i'm left alone with someone
else's thoughts i do not stir or   make noise i listen to dark water
run behind the walls and below me the urkoplad lies dormant waiting
for the next epoch to arrive the antenna trees buzzing with cormorants
there are small things which   escape our attention and lie still
black mold in the cellar pogo-   nip in the forest rats in the cage

LXIII

not faces but black boxes i   permit them anonymity & i get
strong feedback that way i allow their voices to soak through i request
nothing but attention when i   speak so that it seems i speak
alone as if only to myself but sometimes a camera turns on and i'm
startled to find that i'm not   alone that the world continues
beyond the box that it stretches out into human form that it listens

LXIV

let him be immersed there will be no error let him be immersed its tail
neatly above water crossing   the concentric bridge of time let
her be immersed there will be no error let her dictate the event that she
repent of nothing let them be   immersed in error that all error
be immersed in a beauty of accident let the nahual guide my voice when
i sleep in the milpa the matrix   of change lays my shadow to rest

AFTERWORD

The series of poems follows a lyric structure derived from the shape and weight of the hexagrams of the I Ching (易經). However, the poems were not composed according to the traditional method of divination as practiced by the users and consultants of the I Ching, nor are the poems intended to mimic or correlate to acts of cleromancy. They are poems that build upon the recent secular tradition which began with the surrealists and was extended by poets like John Cage and Jackson Mac Low.

The hexagram affords a plenitude, paradoxically, in the infinite nutshell of its constriction. The tensions between the lines, and the pressure points which the reader might discern in the imagery and grammar, in the enjambments and ruptures accidental or forceful, narrate a historical division between the machinic and what Denise Levertov called "organic form." Perhaps there are only two poems in the world, as William Carlos Williams had once implied, machines and anti-machines. These, however, are black boxes. To borrow a resonant phrase from Victor Tausk, these poems are a series of boxes that express themselves in what might be called an "organ language," an artifice of the organism.

A black box can be anything in the sense that anything can fit inside a black box. It can be a system, a machine, a person's mind, an algorithm, a network, an institutional apparatus, a closed-circuit dream. A black box is sealed shut, a hypothetical and impenetrable object, and nothing can be known of what occurs inside. That's the point. What we do see are its inputs and outputs: a set of data, instructions, and materials goes in; people, animals, actions, behaviors, and events come out. But the internal mechanics within the box are completely mythical and speculative. In other words, its chance operations are readable strictly in the lyric mode, in the language of mythological precision.

A breakdown in the black box, or a breakdown occasioned by an escalation in the uncertainties regarding a black box's inventory and functions, is called "black box syndrome." It describes a fatigue prompted by an overwhelming range of positions and possibilities that exceed mathematical modeling and geometrical scaling intended to circumvent breakdowns in the transmission of information and logistical data. In the financial sector, black box syndrome represents the rising volatility of chaos in a managerial system designed to subdue (or simulate) it in the interests of maximizing profit and engineering financial outcomes.

In appropriating "black box syndrome" from its IT and financial contexts, I intend to redefine it as a lyric breakdown that results from the disenchantment of language and the incessant financialization of everyday life. In this sense, the poems attempt to perform a reverse "chaos magic," in which "zones of paranoid infection" (Adorno) are activated through a restrictive, rectangular space of relations and enjambments.

In the I Ching, cleromancy forms the basis of the operation, but like the inner workings of a black box, the procedure resists methodical prediction. Lots are thrown, coins are cast, and numbers are arranged into a hexagram composed of six broken and unbroken lines corresponding to the forces of yin and yang. These actions correspond to a higher order, but its true form is impenetrable by human cognition except through cleromancy, allegory, and hermeneutics. Like astrology and tarot, it is a matter of improvisation and close reading; like astronomy, it is a matter of magnitude, scale, and techne. It is a system for divination, but unlike the divination practices of Wall Street and futures trading, the I Ching stresses cosmological, ethical, and environmental sensitivity and discipline. It is a chaos magic that reorients subjectivity precisely by speaking inside disorientation, at the heart of chaos.

NOTES

Lines and phrases in "What's in the Box" quote and reference *Illustrations of madness: exhibiting a singular case of insanity and a no less remarkable difference in medical opinion ... with a description of the tortures experienced by the patient, James Tilly Matthews, in hallucinations,* by John Haslem, published in London in 1810. The case of James Tilly Matthews is of particular importance for the composition of this book, and multiple poems refer to Matthews' complex theories about the "air loom," an underground machine that he claimed influenced his actions and thoughts from afar. For information about Matthews and John Haslem's text, I referred to Mike Jay's *The Influencing Machine: James Tilly Matthews and the Air Loom* (2003, 2012).

In respect to the psychoanalytic concept of the "influencing machine," which Matthews' air loom seems to mirror and predate, I cite Victor Tausk's "On the Origin of the 'Influencing Machine' in Schizophrenia," an article first published in 1919 (translated by Dorian Feigenbaum). Alongside James Tilly Matthews, Victor Tausk is also a significant figure in the book, and I referenced Paul Roazen's *Brother Animal* for contexts surrounding Tausk's relationship to Sigmund Freud and his fascinating, but tragically short life.

Several terms in the book are drawn from ancient Nahua (Aztec) cosmology, animism, and anatomical science:

tonalli: your fate or destiny according to birth date; your soul and spirit

teyolia: the animistic part of you that journeys to the world of the dead (upon your death or, sometimes, beforehand); also, the heart

ihiyotl: located in the liver, the breath imparted to one upon birth; the breath or air in people that attracts or repels; also, "night air" or "death air," a malign substance that can be sent to attack people

nahual: an affinity that exists between a human being and a living animal in which the destiny of one is shared by the other; in pop cultural parlance, one's "spirit animal"

These terms, their contexts and uses, are taken from Alfredo López Austin's *The Human Body and Ideology: Concepts of the Ancient Nahuas*, translated by Thelma and Bernard Ortiz de Montellano (University of Utha Press, 1980).

All references and citations of the I Ching are drawn from James Legge's translation, The I Ching (Dover, 1963). When necessary, I referenced several online versions of the I Ching to assist with readings.

Hexagram images on pages 16, 18, 87, and 89 are in the public domain and can be sourced to the following links:

https://commons.wikimedia.org/wiki/File:Iching-hexagram-01.png
https://commons.wikimedia.org/wiki/File:Iching-hexagram-61.png
https://commons.wikimedia.org/wiki/File:Iching-hexagram-63.png
https://commons.wikimedia.org/wiki/File:Iching-hexagram-64.svg

Black box image on page 20 is authored by Krauss and in the public domain. This file is licensed under the Creative Commons Attribution-Share Alike 4.0 International license, and its source information is the following:

Krauss, "Blackbox3D-obs.png," 18 December 2014,

https://commons.wikimedia.org/wiki/File:Blackbox3D-obs.png

Book cover was designed by Jose-Luis Moctezuma and it incorporates three images that are in the public domain:

"Diagram of I Ching hexagrams owned by Gottfried Wilhelm Leibniz, 1701," Wikipedia Commons,

https://commons.wikimedia.org/wiki/File:Diagram_of_I_Ching_hexagrams_owned_by_Gottfried_Wilhelm_Leibniz,_1701.jpg

"Utriusque cosmi maioris scilicet et minoris metaphysica, physica atque technica historia ... Tractatus secundus de naturae simia seu technica macrocosmi historia" by Robert Fludd, Wellcome Collection, https://wellcomecollection.org/works/gbbychu2/images?id=gzy3gujm

"Illustrations of madness: exhibiting a singular case of insanity and a no less remarkable difference in medical opinion ... with a description of the tortures experienced by the patient, James Tilly Matthews, in hallucinations" by John Haslam, Wellcome Collection, https://wellcomecollection.org/works/e6n82yw6/images?id=fejvywfz

ACKNOWLEDGMENTS

A selection of poems from *Black Box Syndrome* (XIII-XVII, LI) first appeared in *Spoon River Poetry Review*. My thanks to the editor, Steve Halle, for publishing them.

I first want to thank Rusty Morrison, Laura Joakimson, and the Omnidawn editors for accepting to publish this book and for their invaluable help and feedback on the design of the book. Special words of love and respect are reserved for the memory of Ken Keegan, who had been the person who personally called me on the phone when Omnidawn selected to publish my first book, and whose voice, I remember well, exuded so much warmth and kindness. His presence is sorely missed, but his vision lives on in the work Omnidawn continues to do.

I want to thank Rodrigo Toscano and Edgar Garcia for their tremendous camaraderie, conversation, and critical thinking during the writing of this book. I also want to thank my wife, Mary Lou, who generously and lovingly gave me the space and time to write this book during the dark moments of the pandemic while we raised our family. Lastly, I reserve special thanks to Judith Goldman, whose intellectual support, feedback, and encouragement provided the germ and impetus for the structure of the book. Her particular help on the writing of the "Afterword" was pivotal in giving voice to and articulating the contexts for the book.

Jose-Luis Moctezuma is a Xicano poet based in Chicago. He is the author of a chapbook, *Spring Tlaloc Seance* (Projective Industries, 2016), and *Place-Discipline* (Omnidawn, 2018, and winner of the 1st/2nd Open Poetry Book prize). His poetry and criticism have appeared in *Postmodern Culture, Fence, Jacket2, Chicago Review, Modernism/modernity*, and elsewhere.

Black Box Syndrome
by Jose-Luis Moctezuma

Cover design by Jose-Luis Moctezuma
Cover art from Gottfried Wilhelm Leibniz, Wikipedia Commons, Robert Fludd
and John Haslam, Wellcome Collection

Interior design by Laura Joakimson and Jose-Luis Moctezuma
Cover typeface: Lora
Interior typeface: Lora and Futura

Printed in the United States
by Books International, Dulles, Virginia

Publication of this book was made possible in part by gifts from
Katherine & John Gravendyk in honor of Hillary Gravendyk,
Francesca Bell, Mary Mackey, and The New Place Fund

Omnidawn Publishing
Oakland, California

Staff and Volunteers, Fall 2023
Rusty Morrison, senior editor & co-publisher
Laura Joakimson, executive director & co-publisher
Rob Hendricks, poetry & fiction editor, & post-pub marketing
Jason Bayani, poetry editor
Anthony Cody, poetry editor
Liza Flum, poetry editor
Kimberly Reyes, poetry editor
Sharon Zetter, poetry editor & book designer
Jeffrey Kingman, copy editor
Jennifer Metsker, marketing assistant
Sophia Carr, marketing assistant
Katie Tomzynski, marketing assistant